Steve Bell

CONTENTS

A Methuen Paperback

For Pat and Jim

With thanks to Heather, Brian and Duncan for many ideas and much support.

Special acknowledgements to the artists and writers of the Beanos, Beezers and Dandys of old.

A METHUEN PAPERBACK

This collection first published in Great Britain in 1987
by Methuen London Ltd
11 New Fetter Lane, London EC4P 4EE

Most of the pages in this book published by *City Limits* between 1982 and 1986
Copyright © Steve Bell 1982, 1983, 1984, 1985, 1986, 1987
Introduction © Duncan Campbell 1987

Designed by Brian Homer
Edited by Steve Bell and Brian Homer

Typeset by P & W Typesetters
202 Hagley Road, Edgbaston, Birmingham

Made and printed in Great Britain by
Redwood Burn Ltd., Trowbridge, Wiltshire

British Library Cataloguing in Publication Data

Bell, Steve
   Maggie's farm: the last round up.
   I. Title
   741.5′942   PN6737.B4
   ISBN 0-413-15880-2

A MESSAGE FROM THE FIRST SEA LADY

People often ask me why it is that time after time I agree to write the foreword to Steve Bell's *Maggie's Farm.* After all, they say, each episode of the story is an indictment of my beliefs and policies — this volume deals with the period from 1982 to the present day. Why give credence to such a one-sided version of events?

To them I say this. There are three very good reasons for me to help Steve out in this way.

First of all, Steve is a small businessman. That is to say not 'small' in the physical sense of the word (in fact, he's six foot four and has one of those faces that's clearly never shaken hands with John Razor-Blade) but 'small' in that he works long hours and probably fiddles his VAT bills. He also lives in Sussex. Such people are the lifeblood of our party and our country.

Secondly, he is a satirist. People often ask me, how can I like satire? To them I say — how can a politician who lectures people about the eternal verities of family life and then employs adulterers and divorcees in her cabinet *not* be a satirist? How can someone who talks constantly about the importance of democratic values and then bends over backwards to make sure those values are never implemented in South Africa not be a satirist? You get my drift?

Thirdly, I enjoy a joke as much as the next bloke. I mean, laughter is the best medicine. Put on a happy face. When you're smiling, the whole world smiles with you. You know what I mean? Pack up yer troubles in yer old kit bag and SMILE SMILE SMILE! Happy talky talky, happy talky! You gotta laugh! SMILE THOUGH YOUR HEART IS BREAKING! KEEP SMILING THROUGH! Gotta laugh, eh? Regrets, I had a few . . . I bit them off and spat them out! I CAN TAKE A JOKE! I CAN DO WHAT I LIKE. ME AND RONNIE, WE SHOWED 'EM! WE RULED THE WORLD! EVERY DAY WAS THE FIRST DAY OF SPRING! THAT'S OFFICIAL. GIVE US A SMILE, DARLIN'! Laugh? HAHAHAHAHAHAHAHAHAHAHAHAHHHHHHHHHaaaaaaaaaaaa!

The Mark of the First Minister of Her Brittanic Majesty's Cabinet

Margaret Thatcher was talking to **Duncan Campbell** in a personal capacity. Duncan Campbell was News Editor, *City Limits* 1981-86.

SHOOTOUT ON BEEF MOUNTAIN

CRACK went the automatic weapon of the woman in the armour-plated blue buckskins, and the war whoop of one of the circling Latin Waiters turned to a shriek. "That's one corned-beef-eatin' cur less to deal with!" growled Calamity Thatch, the most daring of all the free-wheelin', gun-runnin' hunger-fighters in the entire Wild West. If there were hungry people anywhere on the range, Calamity Thatch would be there, fighting them. Yet here she was, holed up and pinned down at the Mutton Restaurant on Beef Mountain by an ill-armed band of renegade Latin Waiters, led by the very Meat Magnate she had been running guns to only weeks before. Worse than that; the ammunition was running low and it looked like the end was near for Calamity Thatch. The relief column was still several weeks away.

2—The cunning Latin Waiters knew it. They rained cutlery and flaming napkins on the heads of the plucky defenders. Then they came in with a rush, waving their murderous carving knives and brandishing their spanking new British Army service revolvers. Crawling from beneath a blazing table, Calamity Thatch fought hand-to-hand with the oily demons till she was stunned by a meat tenderiser. At once, a Latin Waiter leapt upon her with a knife.

3—A greasy winkle picker kicked the knife away. "Eeediot!" grated a harsh voice. "Thees eez Calamity Thatch! No easy death for 'er! We 'ave reserved el especial 'oomiliation for 'er!!" Calamity Thatch's wrists were bound, and she was led away. "At last we 'ave won el franchise for el feelthy Eenglayzes Sheeps Restaurant! 'Enceforth eet weel bear the name of 'El Cantina de Bif'!!!" leered the unshaven leader of the Latin Waiters.

4— "You inhuman vermin!" spat Calamity Thatch as she was forced by the cruel waiters to get down on her knees and eat grass in front of her remaining loyal staff of three Half-wits and a wounded Bulldog. "Ha! Now you must eat the grass like yorra estupida sheeps!" sneered the Chief Waiter, "And when you 'ave feeneeshed that you weel be forced to keess the arrass of my prize pet beeg booll, El Bonzo.

5—As Calamity Thatch was pushed towards the El Bonzo's heaving buttocks, seeing her chance to escape she lunged forward, leapt onto its back and dug her heels into its side. The surprised bull galloped off at breakneck speed. "If only I can get word to my friend, the Global Meat Broker and Cute Clown, Ronald Macdonald, then we'll still be in with a fighting chance of winning back the franchise!" She thought to herself.

6— After a long and arduous journey, Calamity Thatch managed to reach an isolated telegraph station, and was able to get a message through to Ronald Macdonald. He responded quickly, and very soon the long-awaited Relief Wagon Train was being flown to Beef Mountain by Burger De-Lite's own heavy air transports. Within weeks, every Latin Waiter, bull and sheep had been wiped off the face of the Mountain in bloody hand-to-hand high explosive hi-tech combat. When the fighting was all over, the three Half-wits and the now recuperating Bulldog were each installed in their own pre-fabricated air-conditioned Five-star Mutton Restaurant, where the gallant lads of the relief column came for really Slap-Up Feeds of Beef Burgers, Beef Kebabs and Beef Wellington. After that Calamity Thatch never looked back. The famous hunger-fighter had won her greatest battle.

THE ATOMIC FISHDOG

©Steve Bell 1987

LIKE a huge silvery thing, the Atomic Fishdog leaped, streaked and swirled as it cleverly herded the fish at the bottom of the North Sea. On the bottom, plucky young Normy Tebbit knelt by the gate of an enormous fish pen as a shoal of young Haddock streaked inside. In the background, Normy's friend, Professor Marshall the scientist beamed as he watched the leaping Fishdog, which he and Young Normy had built. This marvellous mechanical creature could jump, chase, growl, respond to whistles, and do anything a real sheepdog could do, only underwater. Normy was at that moment occupied roping and branding a big Buck Cod, when he noticed a strange mark on the animal's backside.

2—"Look at this! Somebody else has been trying to brand him!" said Normy. Professor Marshall gurgled and rolled his eyes in surprise. Normy continued, "I reckon it's those scheming Smørgasbørd Brothers! They've been trying to steal our stock!" The Smørgasbørd Brothers were a notorious band of Scandiwegian fish rustlers.

3—"If we don't put a stop to this, those Scandiwegian villians will steal every buck in the herd, with all that implies for our national integrity!" So saying, Normy leapt astride the Atomic Fishdog. He put his thumb and forefinger to his helmet and whistled. The Fishdog streaked away with Normy clinging to its steel dorsal fin.

4—After some time, the Atomic Fishdog surfaced at the mouth of the fjord lair of the infamous Smørgasbørd gang. On the bank he could see a group of men brandishing whips. Then he noticed a pen full of fish which the men were whipping into a frenzy.

5—"Hey! Stop that! That's flagrantly in breach of Captain Birdseye's First Law of Fish Processing!!" shouted the plucky lad. "Fjøerk øff, ljittle crjoøepe!" sneered one of the bearded villains, "I djo vøt I vjörnt vid my øwne fjishk!!" "But they're not your fish!" said Normy, "you've stolen them!"

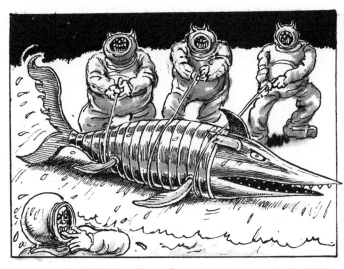

6—"YJENGLÄNDER PJÏGDJØG!!!" With that the burly villains cracked their whips so that they snaked around the helpless Fishdog, pulling it onto the shore and tipping Normy into the water... But Normy wasn't beaten yet. Quick as a flash, he put his fingers to his helmet and gave an ear-piercing whistle.

7—The Atomic Fishdog thrashed its tail, knocking the evil Smørgasbørd Brothers aside like ninepins and breaking the wall of the fishpen, freeing the grateful cod. Next the Fishdog released a foul smelling fluid. "That'll make your fjord uninhabitable by marine life for 50,000 years!" said plucky Normy, grinning at a job well done.

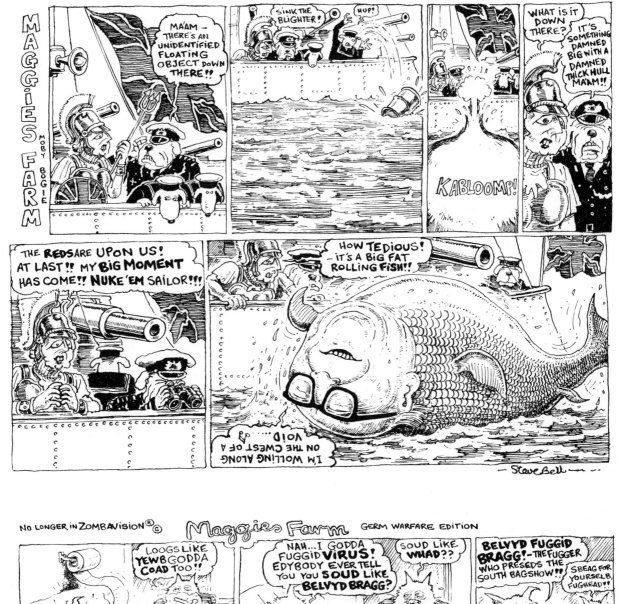

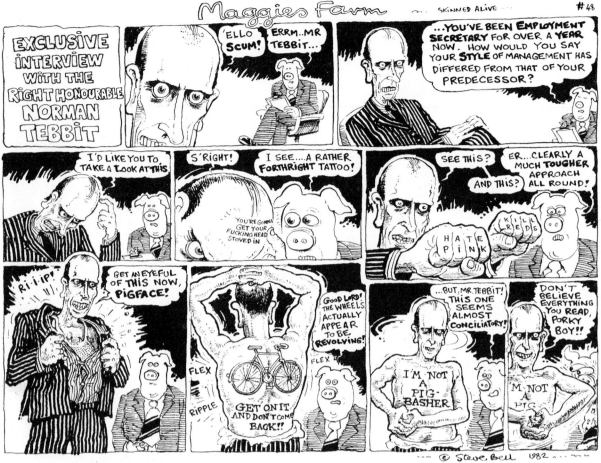

MAGGIE AND HER MAGIC NECK

MAGGIE THATCHER is an ordinary delinquent, ordinary, that is, except for the strange brass bit on her neck.

2—You see, readers, this brass bit was once part of a magic Dreadnought and it gives its owner astounding powers of Public Relations. Maggie has only to give it a rub and she can make anybody believe absolutely anything. Look what happened last June, for instance. Our pal and her friend Cecil were busy earning a bit of extra pocket money by tripping up old fogeys and then giving them back their purses minus a few stray coppers that had "accidentally" slipped into their hands. While they busied themselves with this, Maggie caught sight of Old Mick, a local geriatric, gesticulating at them from across the road. A cheeky smile appeared on Maggie's face. They crossed the road to meet him.

3—"I saw what you did! I'm going to report you to the Police!!" spluttered Old Mick. Maggie smiled and gave her Magic Neck a quick rub. "Yes, we were helping those poor old people, and you'd like to invite us back to your place for a Slap-Up Feed out of sheer gratitude, wouldn't you Old Mick?" she said.
"I...I...I've just had an idea!" gasped Old Mick. "Why don't you young people come back to my place for a Slap-Up Feed?" "Coo, not half!" said Cecil. "That would be terrific fun!" said Maggie. They each took hold of one of Old Mick's hands and ran off down the street, dragging the scruffy old man behind them.

4—By the time they got to his house, Old Mick was at the point of collapse. 'Uuuuuhhuuurrrgghh!'' he wheezed. Maggie gave her Magic Neck a quick rub. "You're feeling really good, and you'd like to get us a huge bottle of pop, wouldn't you?" suggested Maggie, ''Oh, and make yourself a cup of tea while you're at it''. ''Listen, why don't I nip off and get you a huge bottle of pop?'' asked Old Mick. While he was out of the room, Maggie stroked Calley, Old Mick's cat who was sitting purring on the sideboard. ''You'd really like a crap, and you can't be bothered to move off that sideboard, can you?'' Calley obligingly deposited two neat turds on the polished wood surface.

5—When Old Mick returned with a laden tea tray, Maggie said: ''Here, let me be Mother,'' and poured him a cup. She gave her Magic Neck a quick rub. ''You'd like two sugars, wouldn't you, Old Mick?'' and, so saying, she ostentatiously spooned the two cat turds into his cup. ''Brown sugar do you? Here, I can see you're a thirsty man!'' Old Mick gulped down the steaming brew gratefully. Maggie stroked Calley and lightly rubbed her Magic Neck again. ''You're getting hungry, and look! There's a plump young budgerigar perched on Old Mick's head, do you see?'' That cat's eyes gleamed evilly. He tensed, then sprang and sank his claws deep into Old Mick's receding forehead.

6—Old Mick shrieked, reeled and clutched his face. Blood coursed down his forehead. Maggie rubbed her Magic Neck again. ''Looks like everything's coming up rosy for you, in fact, you're so happy you're going to give us all your cash!'' ''Look, why don't you two youngsters go out and buy yourselves a really Slap-Up Feed?'' said Old Mick as he emptied his pockets and wrote them out an enormous cheque. As they walked off laughing, Maggie had another super idea. She beckoned to PC Bloggs who was at that moment passing by. ''I think you should know, Officer, there's an old pervert who's been molesting young people round here. I'll give you his address,'' she said, gently stroking her Magic Neck.

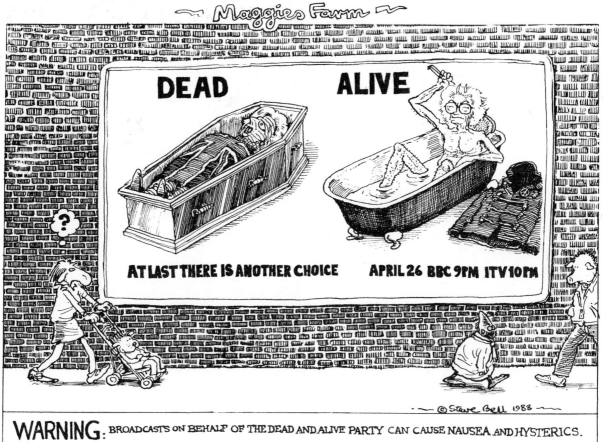

THE BIG PARROT BOY

A HUGE bird wheeled in the air above the grey wastes of rural Berkshire. It was an enormous parrot, and it carried a strange burden. A plucky young lad, clad only in a suit of mottled khaki feathers, was clinging to the bird's scaly legs. He was known as the Big Parrot Boy because of the amazing control he had over his gigantic pet, Polyp. Suddenly, down below, he spotted something that brought a flash of anger to his eyes. "Down, Polyp!" he called. The vast bird flapped its wings and climbed higher into the sky.

2—Half an hour later, the Big Parrot Boy had managed to persuade Polyp to drop him some distance from where he had intended. On the ground the boy could sense danger near at hand. He heard a crashing in the undergrowth, then, he spun round and saw the vicious-looking Big Leader of a pack of evil-smelling Woolly Wimbin. It bared its teeth and shrieked: "Curse you, Big Parrot Boy! We're going to rip your trousers off! Aieeeeeeeeeeeeee!!"

3—Big Parrot Boy made the special call that summoned Polyp. Nothing happened. The Big Leader had just sunk its varnished red claws into the leg of his trousers, when, quite unexpectedly, help arrived. It was his old friend, The Dirty Little Chef. "You look like you could do with a Slap-Up Feed, Big Parrot Boy!" said the Chef, as the whimpering pack of hideous Wimbin cringed back into the evil-smelling undergrowth.

33

ADMIRAL BIMBO

Y OUNG Bimbo Bomgun was one of the luckiest boys in the World. His friend, Professor Von Führerbunker had built the biggest Model Battleship anyone had ever seen. Bimbo had once saved the life of the brilliant scientist von Führerbunker by twiddling the buttons on the wonderful Doomsday Football of tricks that controlled it. It would be a mistake to call the miniature marvel a toy, because it actually possessed the capability to destroy Norwich, or any other medium-sized town. Now 'Admiral' Bimbo was busy demonstrating the model to the incredulous Honduran family down the street.

2—The family were so impressed that they invited Bimbo in for a Slap-Up Feed. As he tucked into the succulent spread, Bimbo said: "Listen, I know you hot-blooded ethnic types are often having Domestic Problems, so why don't you let me and my Model Battleship take care of them for you?" With that, Bimbo very thoughtfully got a squad of his Model Marines to clear the table for the family.

3—Now it so happened that Bimbo knew about a Lebanese family that was having problems on the other side of town. The good-hearted lad decided to pay them a visit with his Model Battleship. "This should help to calm things down a bit," thought Bimbo as his Super Ship lobbed cleverly miniaturised high explosives into their dining room window.

4—Imagine Bimbo's surprise when, instead of the invitation to a Slap-Up Feed he was expecting, one of the wilder members of the family rushed out and brutally stomped on a squadron of Bimbo's Model Marines. Surprise turned to embarrassment when some members of his own family suggested that, perhaps his role as Volunteer Social Worker hadn't been entirely successful.

5—Suddenly he had the most incredible idea. He rushed home and his family were completely bowled over when his miniature shock troops blew out the windows of the Grenadan household next door and occupied the entire house. "I think Black and White should be able to live happily together!" he beamed as he tucked into a Slap-Up Feed at their kitchen table.

41

Daily  Mail

18p

liesMAIL smearsMAIL filthMAIL SPECIAL

I wouldn't wipe my arse with it

By JOSH GOEBBELS

THOUSANDS more people have started playing the 'No Daily Mail' game!

The police don't mind walking the woods all night in a downpour to stop the Greenham women getting themselves shot, or even much mind being spat at and abused on the days when it's tense and ignored when it's quiet.

They don't even mind knowing that most rest days—including the kid's birthday, wedding anniversaries and perhaps Christmas — will be lost to compulsory overtime.

What they dread and find unforgiveable, is being ordered to lay hands on women who often deliberately and calculatingly buy the Daily Mail.

KAK

— NEWS — DIRTY DYKES AND BLACK BASTARDS SHOCK

"I think I deserve a knighthood."

I wouldn't let my dog wipe his arse with it either!

"He must be the luckiest dog alive," said his 21-year-old mistress yesterday.

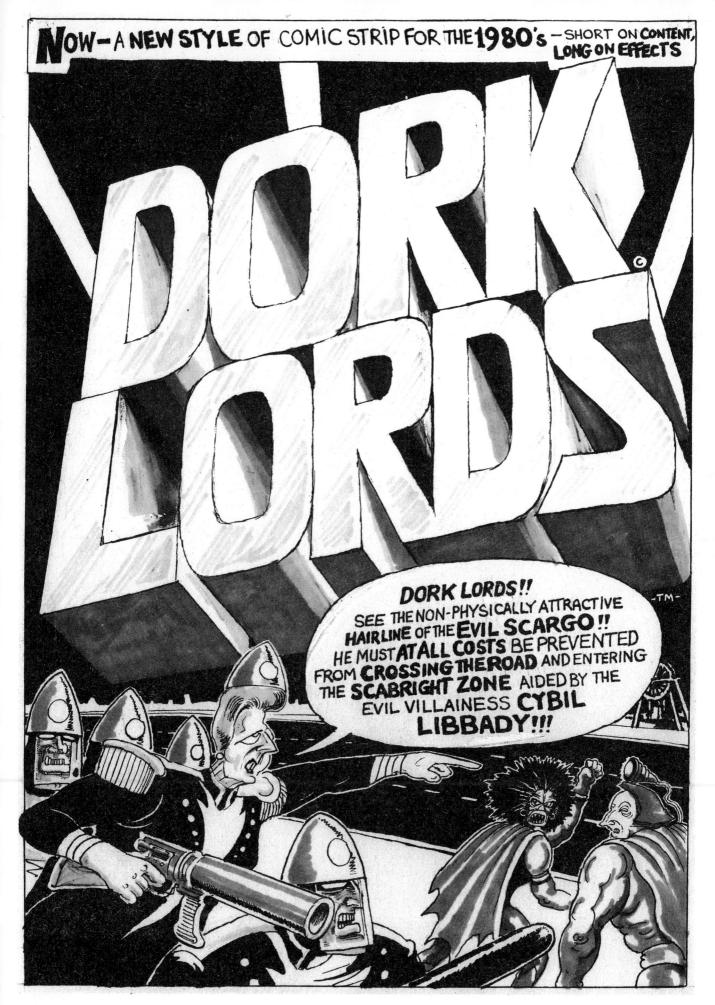

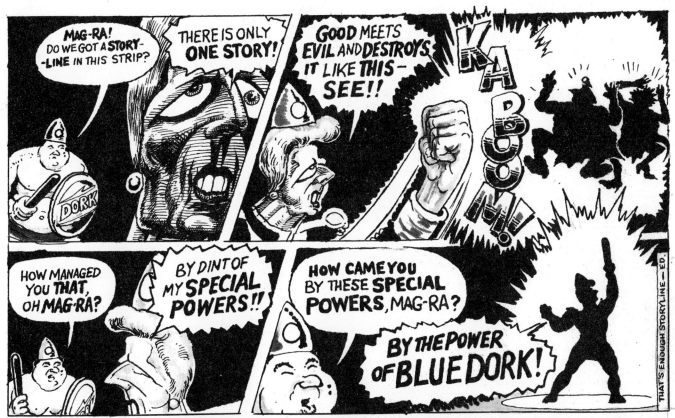

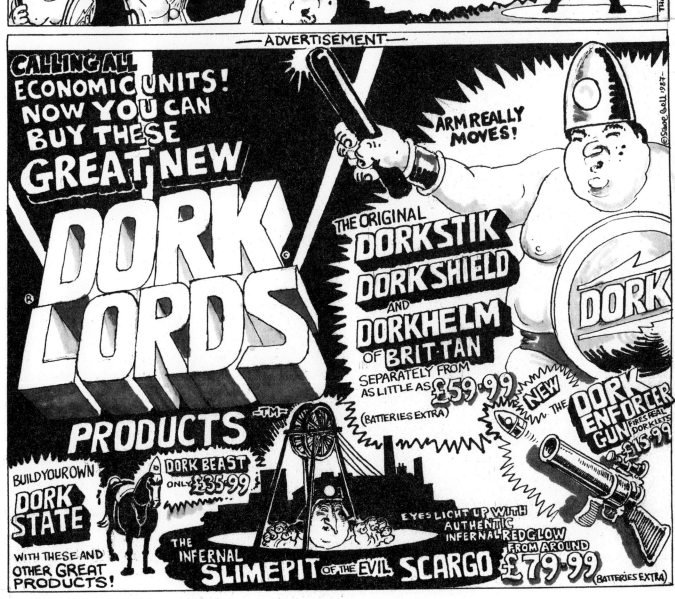

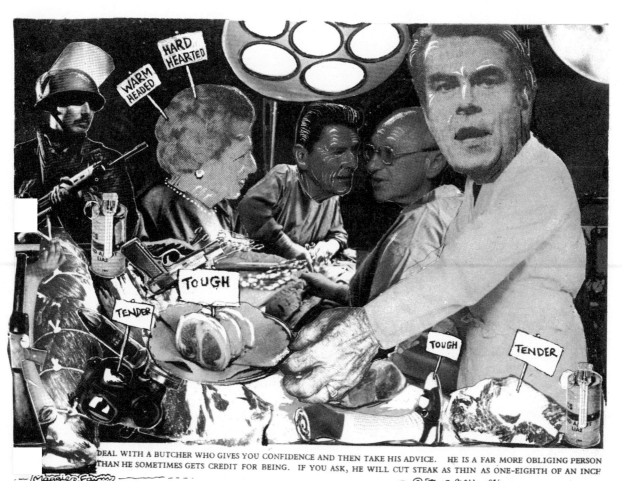

DEAL WITH A BUTCHER WHO GIVES YOU CONFIDENCE AND THEN TAKE HIS ADVICE. HE IS A FAR MORE OBLIGING PERSON THAN HE SOMETIMES GETS CREDIT FOR BEING. IF YOU ASK, HE WILL CUT STEAK AS THIN AS ONE-EIGHTH OF AN INCH

© Steve Bell 1984

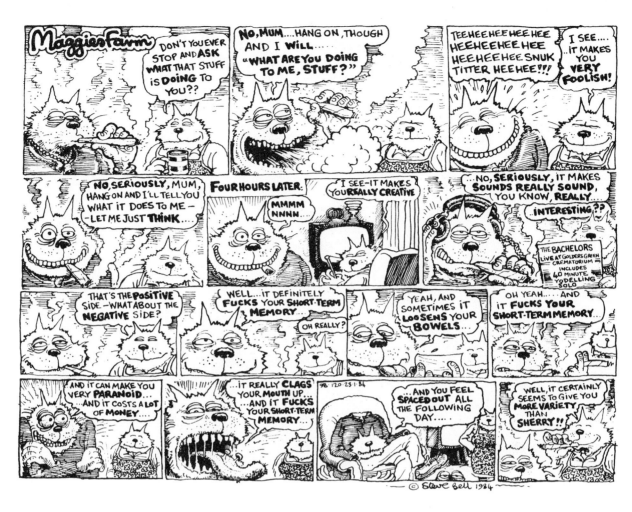

© Steve Bell 1984 — 102 - 19.2.84

53

DON'T LET THIS HAPPEN

ABOLISH PEACE STUDIES NOW

MARK THATCHER

A ROOM OF MY OWN RELATIVE'S

Interviewed by Cecil Parkinson
Photographed by Jean Selwyn Gummer

Mum's command bunker has got everything a growing businessman like me needs. With time at a premium, I need to be able to contact my interests in, say, Hong Kong *fast*. Mum's telecommunications network comes in really handy for that. I'm not the kind of man who's interested in time-wasting nonsense like colour schemes, so the all-round shady battle-ship grey suits me down to the ground.

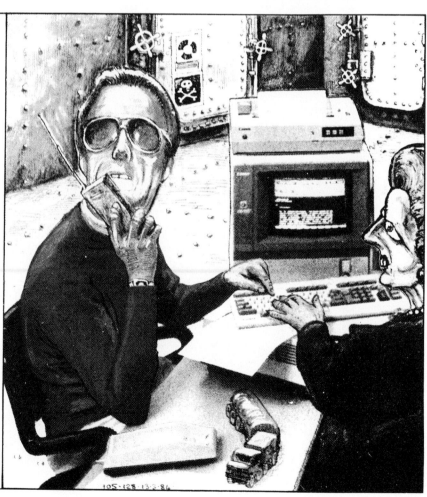

JOHNNY THREE BUTTOCKS

THE HOT SUN beat down on the vast stretch of burning chemical dust that was known as the Great Agribizona Desert. Few men ever ventured into its desolate wastes, but to Johnny Three Buttocks it was home; indeed it had to be because nobody else on the entire Continent wanted to talk to him. Nobody, that is, apart from his faithful dead dog, Spot. To him Johnny Three Buttocks could talk the strange language of the Ancient Agribizonians. Now Johnny stood by a lonely Radish Mountain, sniffing the air intently. "Um problematical climatic negative weather extensification scenario on um way!" he muttered, as great clouds of over-fertilised dust billowed towards him from out of the interior. "Spot, how we responsify to um climatic changification situation?" Spot smiled as always. "Good. We stay um put." said Johnny Three Buttocks, nodding sagely.

2—In a few moments the storm had struck, blotting out everything in choking clouds of dust. Johnny Three Buttocks revised his original plan and began to walk round in circles, clutching his faithful dead hound under his arm. Suddenly, Johnny spotted a ghostly shape looming through the driving dust. Then he realised it was one of the dreaded Benders, erected by a feckless wandering eco-hippy element.

3—Johnny Three Buttocks tensed as a figure reared up out of the makeshift tent. Quivering, Johnny challenged the hairy intruder with the Ancient War Cry of the Agribizonians. "Get orff my land! You parasites just aren't economically viable, by the power of Euro-Skull!"
Quick as lightning, Johnny hurled his stiffened pet at the leering hippy, whose look turned to blank amazement as Spot's sharpened nose pierced him through the heart.

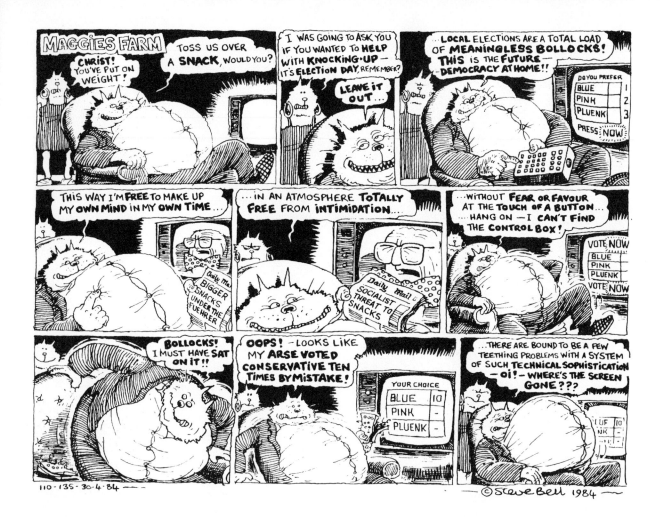

"Goddamn crazy pedestrian pervert!"

NIGEL HOOD
AND HIS MERRY ASSOCIATES

IT WAS a fine sunny day in the Twelfth Century. In a clearing in the forest a lithe, well rounded man in Lincoln Green Pinstripe drew his bowstring taut. A hundred paces off a beggar stood quivering, with a small object tied to the top of his head. "The Snack is mine!" laughed Nigel Hood as his arrow flashed through the air and split the can of Pâté de Foie Gras cleanly down the middle. Cecil Scarlet handed the cheery In-law a foaming tankard of mead, which he downed in one enormous quaff. "We have collected a veritable King's Ransom in Snacks from yon churls!" said Nigel Hood, "All we need now is a King to Ransom. Know ye of any hereabouts?" "There is one to the west of this place who giveth a good return on any collection of stolen Snacks that he receiveth," quoth Little Geoff. But, just at that moment, an arrow struck the tankard out of Nigel Hood's hand.

2— "Shit ye Wattle and Daub!" exclaimed Nigel Hood. "Tis surely the work of the Bastard Black Baron of Barnsley and his Flying Churls! I think ye game could quite conceivably be up!" The band of In-laws began to panic; exclaiming: "Your fault!" "You took 'em, you give 'em back!" "I was just obeying orders!" Then Nigel Hood let forth a great groan of anguish: "Oh Nooooooo! Maid Marion! bring me my Lincoln Brown Pinstriped hose!"

3—Just then a column of Men at Arms, dressed in Lincoln Khaki and Blue appeared. At the head rode the fine squat figure of Leon-A-Dale, Nigel Hood's security consultant, and the beaming but stupid Chief Churl of Nottingham, who said: "I don't agree with these politically motivated strong-arm tactics! Kill the Bastard Black Baron!" "I think this calls for a Slap-Up Banquet!" said Nigel Hood, and everyone gathered round to toast the health of Good King Ron.

DROPPING THE PILOT   AFTER Sir JOHN TENNIEL   DROPPING THE BOLLOCKHEAD — ©Steve Bell 1984

LIZZIE'S BIRTHDAY BOMBSHELL

LIZZIE WINDSOR sighed as she gazed out over that special bit of her backyard they called Horse Guards Parade. It was a lovely hot day in June and it was her birthday, so by rights she should have been cheery as anything. Unfortunately she wasn't; in fact she was downright glum, and the birthday was one of the main reasons for her glumness.

"Why do I have to have an Official Birthday?" she thought to herself. "No one else on this planet has two birthdays. Why should I be the odd one out?"

She knew it was silly to complain. Nobody would have listened, and, if they had, no one would have believed that anyone could possibly not want two birthdays, with two lots of presents, two lots of cards, two lots of treats, two cakes and two really slap-up feeds.

"I'm always having slap-up feeds! I hate slap-up feeds! My life is one long slap-up feed!" she grumbled. The

C.O. of the Household Cavalry looked round in amused surprise.

"I beg your pardon Ma'am? I'm afraid I didn't quite catch…" Lizzie blushed bright scarlet. She couldn't stand the Colonel. His supercilious manner made her feel uneasy at the best of times, and now; to think that he'd just witnessed her talking to herself. She couldn't bear the thought. She was almost beside herself with embarrassment.

"Fuck off big nose! I'll give *you* some real ear'ole if you don't mind yer

own fuckin' business!"

A very loud snorting voice boomed out from below and just in front of where Lizzie was sitting. She looked down in amazement.

The Colonel turned beetroot and concentrated on the inside of his bearskin. There was no one else in the immediate vicinity.

"I tell you it's a fuckin' wind-up, standin' around in this 'eat, gel!" the voice continued. Lizzie leant forward, then suddenly sat bolt upright in the saddle, conscious of the thousands of pairs of eyes scrutinising her every move, some of them, she knew, with powerful binoculars.

"Good God! The new horse! It can talk!" she exclaimed through tightly clenched teeth.

"Let's 'ave a little less of the 'it', gel; I've got me pride y'know. Dobbin is me name, 'orse is me nature, and male is me sexual status. Pleased to meet you I'm sure. I can't shake 'ands at the moment; you know 'ow it is."

"I do indeed," said Lizzie, "but I had no idea that we even had a horse called 'Dobbin'. I think there must have been some mistake!"

"You're another one entcha? Bleedin' Upper Clawsses are all the same: hoity toity buncha fuckin' ponces! Well you can fuck orff ahtavit! Git orff me back! Fuck orff!! Errtcha! I'll show you what I think of your bleedin' parade! Git a load o' this!"

Dobbin stiffened and Lizzie, accomplished horsewoman that she was, raised her weight from the saddle instinctively. A steaming Niagara of horse piss crashed into the dust beneath her. She became even more acutely conscious of the thousands of spectators in their grandstands all around the Horse Guards, and she was absolutely certain she heard a swelling snigger from some way off. "That ain't all, gel!"

There followed immediately a massive explosion of a fart, then a series of staccato "PROOTS!" as, one by one, Dobbin expelled a large number of shiny turds. The sniggering had advanced steadily and was now infecting the troops in her immediate vicinity. Before Lizzie could do anything, Dobbin began to trot sideways, singing in a very loud voice:

'Appy Birthday to you!
'Appy Birthday to you!
'Appy Birthday dear Mon-arch!
'Appy Birthday to you!

"Right! This is where I do the proverbial runner! Arry Viderchy! I'm orff!" Dobbin took off at a gallop. Lizzie had to employ all her considerable resources of horsewomanship to stay in the saddle, but stay on she did; as she clung on to his mane, she ran through as calmly as she could the possible courses of action open to her.

She felt the inside pocket of her tunic for her regulation evening wear service revolver. One bullet through his head now and she could well escape with a few bruises. At that very instant he lurched sideways and broke through the police cordon. He zigzagged towards Trafalgar Square and into the intense traffic. It was much too dangerous to shoot him here. Suddenly he pulled up at a bus stop and tossed Lizzie off his back. She landed in a heap.

"If you think I'm carting you abaht all day you got another think comin'! You can git a Green Line to Windsor from 'ere. See you abaht!"

"Not if my dawgs see you first!" snapped Lizzie.

"Fuck your dawgs, missus; they already 'ad me mother, me father, me sister, me three brothers, not to mention me privates, so they're not gettin' me too! I'm orff!" he shouted as he disappeared into the roaring traffic.

Lizzie took stock of the situation. She was lying in a heap at the foot of a severe looking London Transport Bus Inspector. She felt hot, bothered, filthy dirty and quite out of place in her long black skirt and scarlet tunic. She pulled a dark grey silk scarf out of her pocket and wrapped it around her head. Then she crossed the road.

"I shall have a discreet cup of tea in that Corner Hice over there." she thought to herself.

"Sorry Ma'am, we have a management policy of not servin' 'ippies in this establishment, so fuck off back to Stonehenge!"

A burly figure was blocking the doorway.

She had been on the receiving end of a great deal of bad language that day, but this was the final straw. Centuries of breeding, decades of the most careful and expensive nurturing, training and conditioning broke in that instant.

"Well Fark this for a game of soldiers!!" Her voice echoed out across an unfortunate hush in the traffic noise.

Quite suddenly, magically, Lizzie was back on her horse, standing at attention in the middle of the Horse Guards Parade. The troops were marching past, the crowds were waving their flags. She was aware that she had just taken the salute, but, Oh God, then she remembered. Had she actually said that? The Colonel was looking at her in a most peculiar, one would almost say resentful, way. She leaned forward and looked down at her horse. The dark pool of his eye stared blankly back at her as he dumbly champed his bit.

She straightened up in the saddle and suddenly felt quite despondent. "I suppose this is it," she thought to herself, "this is all there will ever be to my life. I suppose at this point I could either commit suicide, or go and have that slap-up feed. I think I may as well go and have the slap-up feed."

The horse farted appreciatively.

You walk in the door. From now on you're on your own. We put a sack over your head. **We want you to see your future life with us.** Nothing. A blank. You're nothing. Then we give you some white noise, or maybe one of our regular beatings, or a spell with Mr Nasty, or even one with Mr Nice. **There's the kind of variety you just don't get in Civvy Street.** We believe in fitness, so we give you weights. Very heavy weights. You hold one up in front of you till your arms ache, till you cry with the pain, because if you dare to drop it, we'll beat the shit out of you. **You'll be fit** for nothing when we've finished with you, which is probably just as well because you are the enemy. You probably want to join because you can't find a proper job. You probably want to enjoy yourself a bit while you're still young; **You'd like a job that involves Travel.** You're just like all the others. Inside you there's a dirty little subversive, pervert lying, waiting to pour out its heart to a Soviet agent. **We bring the best out of you**, and then we crush it to death. **You'll do** whatever we tell you to do. You'll be nothing. You'll write whatever we tell you to write. You'll be pissing yourself, shitting yourself and screaming like a little stuck pig, screaming for your mummy, screaming for mercy....

....and that's just the interview

Air Force Other Rank

Maggie's Farm © Steve Bell 1985 ~ 147·214·4·11·85

81

Are you ever struck by the unparalleled growth in the number of adverts like this? Who are all these mystery conglomerates and why are they doing so nicely thankyou? Who actually gives a brass fart whether the perpetrators of the latest snack weapon have described their performance with words like Sustained Profit Growth. Progress? I'll tell you who: it's the Double Dinner Fraternity, looking to quadruple the value of their dinner holdings.

JAW
15 STONE 19 STONE 23 STONE 28 STONE 35 STONE 41 STONE 50 STONE +

Nigel Lawson
and friends, getting bigger and cheekier all the time

* Using food lust as a metaphor for cash greed. The author (no sylph) wishes in noway to offend the fat, or those who must eat 2 dinners for medical reasons.

TODAY I AM GOING TO GIVE YOU A **STIFF TALK** ABITE THE MORALITY OF **MODERN DAY PRODUCTION**.

THARTY YAHS AGAY iT WAS ALMOST **IMPOSSIBLE** TO BUY A PAIR OF **FOREIGN** TRIZERS OR SEE A **TAH BLOCK**...

...THEN, ALL OF A SUDDEN THE **LAIR CLASSES** STOPPED WEARING **BRITISH TRIZERS** AND STARTED MOVING INTO **TAH BLOCKS**...

...PRETTY SOON THE **HAME-PRODUCED TRIZER** AND THE **TAIRSED HICE** WERE THINGS OF THE **PAST** AND **GREAT BRITAIN** WAS IN **FULL SCALE DECLINE**.

TODAY WE RECOGNIZE THE **ADVANTAGES OF THE TAIRSED HICE. WHAT**, AFTER ALL, IS **BUCKINGHAM PALACE** IF NOT AN ENORMOUS **TAIRSED HICE**? PEOPLE TODAY WANT TO **AIN THEIR AIN** TAIRSED HISES IN THE SAME WAY AS THEY **AIN THEIR AIN TRIZERS**. PEOPLE WILL **AINLY** CARE ABITE SOMETHING IF THEY **EKSHLY AIN A STAKE** IN IT....

TOO MANY PEOPLE THESE DAYS ARE PREPARED TO ACCEPT **FOURTH RATE NON-COMPETITIVE RENTED NORTHERN INDUSTRIAL TRIZERS**, OR, WHAT IS WORSE, **NAY TRIZERS AT ALL**. IT IS NOT UNTIL PEOPLE ARE PREPARED TO **PURCHASE AN INTEREST** IN THEIR **AIN SMALL TRIZER BUSINESSES**, AS HAPPENS IN **AMERICA**, THAT THIS **SPIRAL OF DECLINING TRIZERS** CAN BE **REVERSED. BELIEVE ME**, I CARE DEEPLY ABITE THE **FUTURE OF THIS COUNTRY** - I HAPPEN TO **AIN HUGE TRACTS** OF IT, NOT TO MENTION **SEVERAL HUNDRED PAIRS OF TRIZERS!** IN FACT, I WOULDN'T BE SURPRISED IF **AIN SEVERAL TAH BLOCKS** AS WELL!! **FUNNY OLD WORLD!** MIND HOW YOU GAY!! DON'T TAKE ANY WOODEN MONEY! AND **PULL YOUR SOCKS UP** YOU DUMBO-LIKE **LITTLE SQUIT** AS MY **OLD DAD** USED TO SAY.....
..RAMBLE..DRON E all WITHOUT VISIBLE JAW MOVEMENTS..

© Steve Bell 1985 —— 149·218·2·12·85 - - -

THE PROONS

WITH SINCERE APOLOGIES TO DUDLEY D. WATKINS

PAW—HOV YE SEEN GRANPAW THE DAY?

HE'S OOT DOON THE CLUB!!

HE'S ALLUS DOON THAT CLUB! WHIT AH WANTAE KNOW IS WHETHER HE'LL BE IN FER TEA OR NO... OCH! HERE HE IS NOO!

HOW'S IT GOIN', GRANPAW? HOW'S THINGS DOON AT THE PINK FLAMINGO!

AH'M TELLIN' YE—LIFE IN THIS TOON'S NO BEEN THE SAME FOR ME SINCE AH DECIDED TAE COME OOT LAST YEAR!

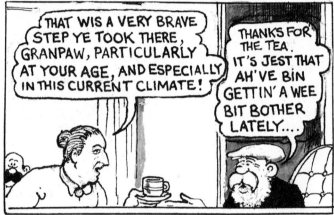

THAT WIS A VERY BRAVE STEP YE TOOK THERE, GRANPAW, PARTICULARLY AT YOUR AGE, AND ESPECIALLY IN THIS CURRENT CLIMATE!

THANKS FOR THE TEA. IT'S JEST THAT AH'VE BIN GETTIN' A WEE BIT BOTHER LATELY....

BOTHER? WHO'S BEEN GIE'IN' YE BOTHER, GRANPAW? IS IT THE BOYS? IS IT PAW HERE?

OCH, NO, THEY'VE ALL BEEN VERY UNDERSTAUNDIN'—NO, AH'VE BEEN GETTIN' A BIT O' TROUBLE FROM THE MINISTER, AN' A BIT MAIR FROM THE POLIS.....

...AND A LOT O' CRAP FROM YON FAMILY ACROSS THE STREET. SHE WILLNAE LET ME GIE HER WEANS ONY O' MA SPECIAL MINTS. AH ALWAYS USED TAE GIE 'EM MA MINTS, SO IT'S NO AS IF THEY DINNA KNOW ME!

ACH! THAT WHITEHOOSE IS NOCHT BUT A BIGOTED AULD BIZZOM!

...AS FER THE POLIS—WELL, WHIT D'YE EXPECT FROM THEM THESE DAYS? THEY'RE A' O'ERPAID AN' IN THRALL TAE THARCHER. BUT THE MINISTER! NOO THAT'S DIFFERENT! HE CALLS HISSELF A MAUN O' GOD!

AH'M GAUNTAE GO AN' HOV IT OOT WI' HIM—YOUSE CAN GET YERSELVES YER AIN SUPPER THE NICHT!

DINNAE WORRY MAW—AH'M TAKIN THE BOY DOON THE DISCO!!

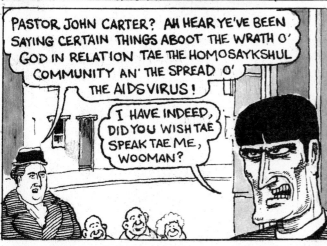

DRAMATIC RECONSTRUCTION of Leon Brittan opening his lunch and failing to resign last week.
(Left to Right) Sir Robert Armstrong (Cabinet Secretary); Margaret Thatcher; Lord Whitelaw; Leon Brittan; Norman Fowler;
Keith Joseph; Norman Tebbit; the Sultan of Brunei; Nigel Lawson; Mark Thatcher; P.W. Botha; Lord Young; —151·225·20·1·86—

TOGETHER AT LAST IN ONE GREAT HI-TECH PACKAGE

THE **Sun** TIMES

MONDAY FEBRUARY 3 1986   25p

PRINT SHIT SLAVES HORROR

Papa Murdoc clamps down on foreign press

Foreign reporters covering protests against the regime of President "Papa **Mr Rupert MurDoc**", have been restricted to the capital of Port-au-**London** where the **electricians' union** were patroling the streets with other security forces yesterday. The Information Minister, Mr Douglas Hurd said yesterday that they would not be allowed to travel into the interior.

In another development, a partial daytime curfew was imposed in the north coast city of Manchester a focal point of protests, BBC **Radio London** the government owned radio station, reported.

The Government also ordered all owners of radio transmitters to report their location to authorities. It was the first use of the curfew since President **Murdoc** declared a state of siege on Friday. The protests erupted at dawn on Saturday in Cap **Wapping** according to reports received here by the US Embassy. Protesters clashed with security forces, who fired shots and used tear gas.

Wapping was in the balance yesterday, the atmosphere sullen, pregnant and oppres-sive, as in the prelude to a thunderstorm. Bursts of rifle and machine gunfire punctuated the night in the capital. There was an extraordinary mingling of hope and apprehension among the people, a belief that at long last something was happening, that the days of the house of **Murdoc** are numbered.

For nearly 27 years the ConCon Macoute have oppressed this country and reduced its 5 5 million people to penury and the indignity of being the poorest country in the Western hemisphere. "Baby Duke" Edinburgh who has known no trade other than that of dick , his good-looking, hard-spending wife Queen and the rest of the small Royal elite, have a careless style and attitude that is plainly a monstrous affront to the ground-down people.

The ConCon regime is today weighed down by its own preposterousness and undermined by the resentment of a people who feel they have endured long enough. The mood springs from hunger and a rotting economy, from a growing sense of injustice and a realization of what the ConCons have taken over the years.

THIS WEEK IN YOUR TEARAWAY TIMES

Love secrets of the + WAFEREaters

PALAZZO DEL DOLE SCROUNGERS IN BLOCKED TRAFFIC OUTRAGE

SEX SECRETS OF THE HAT FETISHISTS

'IT'S JUST A SCAM TO UP MY CIVIL LIST HAND-OUT' ADMITS 'DUKE OF SEX'

GREAT GREAT GREAT GREAT GREAT GRANDFATHER 'WAS OUTRIGHT NUTTER' SHOCK

FIRST FAMILY OF FREEBIEDOM CONFESS 'WE NEED THE MONEY BECAUSE WE DO A LOT OF HORSE'